Investigations

Sliding

Patricia Whitehouse

www.raintreepublishers.co.uk
Visit our website to find out more information about **Raintree** books.

To order:
☎ Phone 44 (0) 1865 888112
▤ Send a fax to 44 (0) 1865 314091
▢ Visit the Raintree Bookshop at **www.raintreepublishers.co.uk** to browse our catalogue and order online.

First published in Great Britain by Raintree,
Halley Court, Jordan Hill, Oxford OX2 8EJ,
part of Harcourt Education.
Raintree is a registered trademark of Harcourt
Education Ltd.

Editorial: Nick Hunter and Diyan Leake
Design: Michelle Lisseter
Picture Research: Beth Chisholm
Production: Lorraine Hicks

Originated by Dot Gradations
Printed and bound in China by South China
Printing Company

ISBN 1 844 21554 7 (hardback)
07 06 05 04 03
10 9 8 7 6 5 4 3 2 1

ISBN 1 844 21560 1 (paperback)
08 07 06 05 04
10 9 8 7 6 5 4 3 2 1

British Library Cataloguing in Publication Data
Whitehouse, Patricia
Sliding
531.1'1
A full catalogue record for this book is available
from the British Library.

Acknowledgements
The publishers would like to thank the
following for permission to reproduce
photographs: Corbis/Mug Shots, **5**; Heinemann
Library/Que-Net, **4, 6, 7, 8, 9, 10, 11, 12, 13,
14, 15, 16, 17, 18, 19, 20, 21, 22, 23, 24**

Cover photograph reproduced with permission
of Heinemann Library/Que-net.

Every effort has been made to contact copyright
holders of any material reproduced in this book.
Any omissions will be rectified in subsequent
printings if notice is given to the publishers.

Some words are shown in bold, **like this**. They are explained in the glossary on page 23.

Contents

What is sliding?

Sliding is one way of moving.

You are sliding when you go down a slide.

Some **surfaces** are good for sliding.

Some surfaces are not.

What surfaces are good for sliding?

ice

Put a **brick** on some **smooth** ice.

Gently push the brick.

The brick slides on the smooth ice.

Ice is a good **surface** for sliding.

Put a **brick** in some sand.

Can it slide now?

The brick gets stuck in the soft sand.

Sand is not a good **surface**
for sliding.

Does everything slide well on a smooth surface?

This hard floor is **smooth**.

Socks are smooth, too.

The socks and the floor slide against each other.

These shoes are **rough** on the bottom.

Can they slide on the **smooth** floor?

Rough things do not slide well on smooth **surfaces**.

Can you make something slide?

This plastic jar is full of water.

Can it slide on the **rough** wood?

Gently push the jar on the wood.

It does not slide.

Pour some washing-up liquid on to the wood.

Now what happens when you push the jar?

The jar slides.

The washing-up liquid makes the wood **slippery**.

How can water help you slide?

Your swimming costume is **smooth**, and the dry plastic is smooth.

Can you slide?

You can slide on the plastic,
but not very much.

Spray water on the plastic.

Water makes the plastic **slippery**.

Wet, slippery **surfaces** are good for sliding.

Now you can slide!

Quiz

Which **surface** is more **slippery**?

Look for the answer on page 24.

Glossary

brick
hard pieces of baked clay used for building

rough
uneven or bumpy surface

slippery
very smooth and easy to slip on

smooth
even surface that is not bumpy or rough

surface
the top part of something, like a floor or worktop

Index

Answer to quiz on page 22

The wet, soapy floor is a more slippery surface. Be careful!

 CAUTION: Children should not attempt any experiment without an adult's help and permission.